D1168477

PROFILES IN MATHEMATICS

Sophie Germain

Profiles in Mathematics:

Sophie Germain

Stephen Ornes

PUBLISHING

Greensboro, North Carolina

Profiles in Mathematics:

Alan Turing
Rene' Descartes
Carl Friedrich Gauss
Sophie Germain
Pierre de Fermat
Ancient Mathematicians
Women Mathematicians

PROFILES IN MATHEMATICS
SOPHIE GERMAIN

Copyright © 2009 By Stephen Ornes

All rights reserved.
This book, or parts thereof, may not be reproduced in any form
except by written consent of the publisher. For more information write:
Morgan Reynolds Publishing, Inc., 620 South Elm Street, Suite 223
Greensboro, North Carolina 27406 USA

Library of Congress Cataloging-in-Publication Data

Ornes, Stephen.
  Sophie Germain / by Stephen Ornes.
    p. cm. -- (Profiles in mathematics)
  Includes bibliographical references and index.
  ISBN-13: 978-1-59935-062-2
  ISBN-10: 1-59935-062-9
  1. Germain, Sophie, 1776-1831. 2. Mathematicians--France--Biography.
3.
Women mathematicians--France--Biography. I. Title.
  QA29.G468O76 2008
  510.92--dc22
  [B]

                              2008012287

Printed in the United States of America
First Edition

NOV 1 4 2000

Contents

Introduction

Mathematics gives us a powerful way to analyze and try to understand many of the things we observe around us, from the spread of epidemics and the orbit of planets, to grade point averages and the distance between cities. Mathematics also has been used to search for spiritual truth, as well as the more abstract question of what is knowledge itself.

Perhaps the most intriguing question about mathematics is where does it come from? Is it discovered, or is it invented? Does nature order the world by mathematical principles, and the mathematician's job is to uncover this underlying system? Or is mathematics created by mathematicians as developing cultures and technologies require it? This unanswerable question has intrigued mathematicians and scientists for thousands of years and is at the heart of this new series of biographies.

The development of mathematical knowledge has progressed, in fits and starts, for thousands of years. People from various areas and cultures have discovered new mathematical concepts and devised complex systems of algorithms and equations that have both practical and philosophical impact.

To learn more of the history of mathematics is to encounter some of the greatest minds in human history. Regardless of whether they were discoverers or inventors, these fascinating lives are filled with countless memorable stories—stories filled with the same tragedy, triumph, and persistence of genius as that of the world's great writers, artists, and musicians.

Knowledge of Pythagoras, René Descartes, Carl Friedrich Gauss, Sophie Germain, Alan Turing, and others will help to lift mathematics off the page and out of the calculator, and into the minds and imaginations of readers. As mathematics becomes more and more ingrained in our day-to-day lives, awakening students to its history becomes especially important.

Sharon F. Doorasamy
Editor in chief

Editorial Consultant

In his youth, Curt Gabrielson was inspired by reading the biographies of dozens of great mathematicians and scientists. "I was driven to learn math when I was young, because math is the language of physical science," says Curt, who named his dog Archimedes. "I now know also that it stands alone, beautiful and mysterious." He learned the more practical side of mathematics growing up on his family's hog farm in Missouri, designing and building structures, fixing electrical systems and machines, and planning for the yearly crops.

After earning a BS in physics from MIT and working at the San Francisco Exploratorium for several years, Curt spent two years in China teaching English, science, and math, and two years in Timor-Leste, one of the world's newest democracies, helping to create the first physics department at the country's National University, as well as a national teacher-training program. In 1997, he spearheaded the Watsonville Science Workshop in northern California, which has earned him recognition from the U.S. Congress, the California State Assembly, and the national Association of Mexican American educators. Mathematics instruction at the Workshop includes games, puzzles, geometric construction, and abacuses.

Curt Gabrielson is the author of several journal articles, as well as the book *Stomp Rockets, Catapults, and Kaleidoscopes: 30+ Amazing Science Projects You Can Build for Less than $1.*

Sophie Germain

one
Finding
Inspiration

As a child, Sophie Germain often had to resort to extremes to follow her passion. On frosty winter nights near the end of the eighteenth century, she frequently rose from her bed and wrapped herself in blankets. While the rest of her family slept soundly in their beds, she huddled over a desk and worked on math problems. Sophie was forced to conduct her studies at night and in secret because her parents did everything they could to discourage her from delving into mathematics. At the time, it was believed that females did not possess the mental faculties necessary to understand the intricacies of complicated subjects such as math and science, and these subjects were considered inappropriate for girls. But Sophie had a burning desire to learn.

Without a teacher or tutor, recalled her friend Guglielmo Libri, she toiled in her father's library, overcoming "all obstacles which her family first tried to impede so extraordinary a taste for her age, no less than for her sex, by getting up at night in a room so cold that the ink often froze in its well, working enveloped with covers by the light of a lamp even when, in order to force her to rest, her parents had put out the fire and removed her blankets and a candle from the room."

Her father's collection of books contained volumes on many different subjects but it was mathematics that Sophie was drawn to. She was reported to be shy and awkward in social situations, but when it came to math, she was anything but timid. She embraced her work with a fervor and stubbornness that bordered on obsession. More than once her worried parents caught her studying by candlelight, and they pleaded with her to stop her nocturnal routine and get adequate rest.

Yet neither her parents' badgering nor societal conventions could quell her interest. She worked diligently through a book called *Complete Course in Mathematics*, by Etienne Bezout, teaching herself the basics of the subject night after night. As Libri related, it was after one of these nights that her parents woke in the morning to find their young daughter sound asleep at her desk, pen in hand, with the ink frozen solidly in its well. Only sleep, it seemed, could separate the young intellectual from her studies.

Her parents could never have known their sleeping daughter would grow up to become one of the most influential mathematicians of her generation, garnering national prizes and accolades. Without Sophie Germain's work on vibrations, engineers would not have been able to build the Eiffel Tower. And her most important studies—which examined ways that numbers relate to each other—ultimately contributed to the solution of the most famous unsolved problem in math history. Through stubborn will and creativity, she excelled in a time and place that suppressed the higher education of women.

Born April 1, 1776, Marie-Sophie Germain was the middle of three daughters of Ambroise-François and Marie-Madeleine Germain. Ambroise Germain, a wealthy silk merchant, would later attain a high position in the French government. Not much is known about Sophie's mother.

Sophie grew up in an apartment above the family's store on rue St. Denis in Paris. War with foreign countries and social upheaval inside France formed the backdrop of her childhood years. When she was two, France declared war on Great Britain in support of the rebellious American colonies. Violence struck much closer to home the year Sophie turned thirteen. In July 1789, rioters unhappy with France's king stormed the Bastille, a prison located slightly more than a mile from the Germains' house. About a hundred people died in the fighting.

Over the succeeding years, during Sophie Germain's adolescence, the French Revolution would witness much greater bloodshed. It was during this tumultuous time that Sophie found her calling in the world of mathematics. Her father's library provided a safe haven, far away from the brutality of the Revolution. Curious and shy, Sophie read many volumes in the room. The same year the Bastille fell, she came across a book titled *History of Mathematics*, by Jean-Étienne Montucla. Published in 1758, Montucla's book had quickly achieved widespread popularity. It gave ordinary folk a window into the world of mathematics and mathematicians. Sophie was immediately inspired, Guglielmo Libri later reported, when she read Montucla's entry for Archimedes.

Archimedes *(Courtesy of Roger Viollet Collection/Getty Images)*

Born around 287 BCE, Archimedes was one of the greatest mathematicians and scientists of the ancient world. A native of the Greek city of Syracuse, on the island of Sicily, he was renowned throughout the Mediterranean region. His many inventions included a planetarium and a water screw, a device that could transport water uphill. In mathematics, among many other innovations and proofs, Archimedes developed a way of determining the area under a given curve. His method is now regarded as a cornerstone in the development of integral calculus, a vitally practical field of mathematics that enjoyed significant development nearly 2,000 years later.

An ardent scholar, Archimedes dedicated himself so thoroughly to the abstract world of mathematics that he often did not take notice of the everyday world around him. It was said that he sometimes became so engrossed in thought that he forgot to eat and drink, and his servants would have to insist that he take nourishment.

Archimedes lived in a city besieged by war, and Sophie Germain only had to look out her window to glimpse violent conflict. Archimedes' dedication to mathematics, and his tendency to tune out the strife-filled world around him, found a sympathetic soul in Sophie.

Yet it was not simply Archimedes' life that inspired young Sophie Germain. The extraordinary circumstances of his death, recounted by ancient writers such as Plutarch and Cicero, also made a deep impression.

For most of his life, Archimedes lived in Syracuse, which was caught between two rival powers: Rome and Carthage. By the middle of the third century BCE, Syracuse had come under Roman domination and was compelled to pay taxes to Rome. In 213, however, pro-Carthaginian factions in the city began to revolt against Roman authority. In response, Rome sent General Marcus Claudius Marcellus to invade Syracuse. Marcellus gave his soldiers free rein to pillage the city and slay any inhabitants who crossed their paths—anyone, that is, except the famous Archimedes. Marcellus deeply admired the work of the famous mathematician.

Through either ignorance or defiance, the Roman soldier who went to the home of Archimedes did not follow orders. Historians suggest that the soldier did not recognize the mathematician and that Archimedes, consumed with drawing geometric figures in the sand floor, barely noticed that someone had entered his home. When he became aware of the soldier's presence—perhaps he saw a boot near his hand or perhaps the wind changed—he said, "I beg you, don't disturb this." But the Roman soldier struck him down, and the great mathematician died seconds later.

These ancient accounts depict Archimedes as a mathematician whose devotion to learning trumped even his survival instincts. His example led Sophie Germain to realize that succeeding in mathematics required a single-minded effort. As a young woman growing up in a culture that discouraged women from difficult intellectual pursuits, she knew that her path would be even more arduous.

Sophie by no means focused exclusively on mathematics. "Mademoiselle Germain . . . mastered different areas of knowledge, any one of which would have established the reputation of a woman," Libri wrote. "She was very competent in the natural sciences. Then too, she had learned Latin on her own, not for its own sake, since in her view languages were only instruments of study, but in order to enable her to understand diverse works, notably those of Newton and Euler."

The English scientist Isaac Newton, who died nearly fifty years before Sophie Germain was born, studied the properties of light and of motion. His equations of motion allowed physicists to explain how the planets orbit the sun and why cannonballs follow a rainbowlike arc as they fly through the sky. Newton also helped develop calculus. This field of mathematics has two essential components, derivatives and integrals, which use infinitesimally small measurements to execute calculations. Derivative calculus concerns how one quantity changes with respect to another variable—for example, how a bicyclist's speed changes as time passes, or how the volume of a balloon changes as it deflates. Integral calculus is a sophisticated method of addition that helps math-

Germain taught herself Latin in order to study the works of Isaac Newton. *(Courtesy of Old Paper Studios/Alamy)*

ematicians calculate lengths, areas, and volumes. Calculus is one of the most important tools required of a serious mathematics student.

Like Newton, the celebrated Swiss mathematician Leonhard Euler (pronounced *OIL-er*) made great advances in both physics and mathematics. The father of thirteen children, Euler still managed to find the time to publish more than eight hundred papers. His contributions to mathematics range across many different areas. In particular, Sophie Germain was captivated by his thoughts and work in number theory—an area of math

Leonhard Euler

concerned with the properties of integers (whole numbers, the negatives of those numbers, and zero).

Among his other accomplishments, Euler used a method first introduced by Archimedes to demonstrate that there are infinitely many prime numbers. Prime numbers are numbers divisible only by themselves and by one. Five and seven, for example, are prime numbers. Primes are particularly interesting to mathematicians because they seem to occur at random on the number line. Euler wrote, "Mathematicians have tried in vain to this day to discover some order in the sequence of prime numbers, and we have reason to believe that it is a mystery into which the human mind will never penetrate."

Sophie also took interest in Euler's work on differential equations—that is, equations that rigorously describe the way a function changes. Differential equations provide mathematicians with a helpful way to use math to describe complicated natural phenomena, like the way water flows through a pipe, or the way air moves around a flying airplane.

Sophie knew that to pursue a career in mathematics, she would have to familiarize herself with the work of Newton, Euler, and many others who had made fundamental advances in the field. For years, she toiled furtively at night, determined to learn as much as she could as quickly as possible.

Eventually, Sophie Germain's parents recognized that their efforts to suppress her interest in mathematics were no match for her zeal. If their quiet and studious young daughter wanted to become a mathematician, then they would support her. They did, in fact, make certain she was provided for her entire life.

Relieved of having to pursue her passion in private, Sophie Germain set out to learn as much as she could in the light of day. Soon her father's library, as large as it was, began to prove inadequate to satisfy her curiosity. She needed a deeper, more thorough education than the one she was giving herself. But just as she was outgrowing the library, war-torn France spiraled into disorder and confusion.

Since 1789, some citizens had sought to replace the French monarchy with a more representative form of government. Ambroise Germain was one such person; he frequently hosted gatherings of reform-minded citizens at his house. In June of 1791, amid growing discontent with his regime, King Louis

XVI had attempted to flee France with his family. The royal family was arrested and returned to Paris, however. By the following year, the monarchy had been overthrown, and the revolutionary government beheaded the former king at the guillotine in January 1793. The unpopular former queen, Marie-Antoinette, was executed that October.

Yet the toppling of the monarchy failed to bring stability and peace. Revolutionary factions battled each other for power. Mob violence erupted frequently. France declared war on Austria, then Great Britain, the Netherlands, and Spain—all of which opposed the French Revolution's republican principles. Within France, the months between September 1793 and July 1794 were especially bloody. During this period,

A mob storms the Bastille in Paris during the French Revolution. Germain sought refuge among the books in her father's library during the turbulent revolution. *(Courtesy of MPI/Getty Images)*

which became known as the Reign of Terror, the group that had seized control of the government set about executing real or imagined enemies of the Revolution. As many as 40,000 French citizens were beheaded by means of the guillotine. The Place de la Révolution, the location of these public executions, was fewer than two miles from the home of Sophie Germain and her family.

Yet despite the violence and bloodshed in the streets of Paris, the French Revolution also ushered in an era of unprecedented growth in mathematics. In 1794, intellectuals in Paris founded a school, the École Polytechnique, that attracted great scientific minds to teach and do research.

For Sophie Germain, who was eager to continue her studies, the founding of the Polytechnique was both fortuitous and cruel: while the school would have been the ideal place for her to pursue mathematics, women were not welcome to walk its halls or take classes from its esteemed professors. But the exclusionary rules of the École Polytechnique would prove to be no match for the persistence of Sophie Germain.

two
Monsieur LeBlanc and Professor Lagrange

France was undergoing a dramatic political and social transformation as Sophie Germain became a young woman, but this was not the only change she witnessed during this period. Her father was elected to an important government position. Her older sister, Marie-Madeleine, married a man named Charles Lherbette and in 1791 gave birth to her only child. This son, Jacques-Amant Lherbette, would become a lawyer and politician. He remained close to Sophie his entire life.

But perhaps most important from Sophie's point of view, the educational climate of Paris was changing. The spirit of revolution had spread to the schools, and a new philosophy of education was taking hold among the scientific elite. New schools were established with goals that were not served by the older institutions. The founding of the École Polytechnique (originally named the École Centrale des Travaux Publics) and its sister school, the École Normale, offered an alternative to the institutions that formerly had been used to prepare young men for military service. These new universities represented a fresh approach to higher education. Before this time, scientists and mathematicians worked exclusively in scientific academies, sequestered from the rest of the world;

Students at the École Polytechnique (*Courtesy of Hulton Archive/Getty Images*)

ARMÉE FRANÇAISE

ÉCOLE POLYTECHNIQUE

university classes, meanwhile, were taught by instructors who were not necessarily experts in their fields.

By contrast, at the École Polytechnique—which represented the pinnacle of France's educational system—top scientists became teachers. The eminent thinkers of the time stood in the front of lecture halls, presenting and explaining their original work. Mathematics and science were the dominant subjects at the Polytechnique, and the educators and students who populated the school in its early years would become the pioneers of a new branch of mathematics called "mathematical physics." They included Siméon-Denis Poisson, Jean-Baptiste-Joseph Fourier, and Pierre-Simon de Laplace.

In keeping with the ideals of the French Revolution, France's new educational system was intended to be more democratic: theoretically, it promised through virtue of knowledge and expertise to help men of lower social and financial status rise professionally. Of course, higher education remained closed to women.

Nevertheless, the opportunity to study under the greatest scientists of her time proved irresistible for Sophie Germain. Through a series of events both tragic and fortuitous, she managed to penetrate the forbidden corridors of the École Polytechnique.

Shortly after the school opened, she met a young man named Antoine-August LeBlanc. LeBlanc, who was enrolled in the École Polytechnique's first class, shared the lecture notes from his classes with Germain. Soon, however, he was called away to military service, and he died at the age of twenty-two.

But that was not the end of his story. LeBlanc had not notified the administration of the École Polytechnique that

Pierre-Simon de Laplace studied science and math at the Polytechnique, and became a pioneer in a new branch of mathematics called "mathematical physics." *(Courtesy of Hulton Archive/Getty Images)*

he was leaving, and his departure and tragic death provided Sophie Germain with an unusual opportunity. She continued to receive lecture notes the school printed for Antoine-August LeBlanc, and in 1795 or 1796, she began to submit written work to the École Polytechnique under his name.

In this manner, she was able to greatly advance her education. For example, she gained access to the chemistry lessons of Antoine-Françoise de Fourcroy, a doctor who helped pioneer the study of plant and animal chemistry. More important,

Using a pseudonym, Germain took chemistry lessons from Antoine-Françoise de Fourcroy, a doctor who helped pioneer the study of plant and animal chemistry. *(Courtesy of Visual Arts Library (London)/Alamy)*

she was exposed to some sophisticated mathematical tools, including a new type of differential equations.

Ordinary differential equations express rates of change in a system and are easily applied to real-world situations. Partial differential equations allow for a finer-tuned analysis; they enable mathematicians and physicists to study the way a system changes as a result of just one of its variables. The study of sound (acoustics) and the study of liquids, for example, both incorporate partial differential equations. Scientists also use these equations to create mathematical models for turbulent weather patterns.

Under her assumed identity of Antoine LeBlanc, Sophie Germain was again studying mathematics in secret, by her own rules. For her, learning was paramount; she did not care whether she received accolades for her accomplishments. "This forgetting of self she displayed in all her activities," her friend Guglielmo Libri would recall. "It was evident in science, which she cultivated with a complete denial of self, never thinking of the advantages that success procures."

Still, because she was secretly circumventing the École Polytechnique's ban on female students, Germain's mathematics training was somewhat haphazard. She did not have access to all of the institution's resources, and she lacked a mentor from its faculty. As a result, her instruction in the basics did not follow the usual path of students of mathematics, and she lacked some rudimentary skills. Paradoxically, Germain's unorthodox training would later prove to be her greatest asset.

Ultimately, Germain's charade unraveled because of a university requirement. At the end of each course at the École Polytechnique, professors assigned their students to submit written observations and research. When a distinguished mathematics professor named Joseph-Louis Lagrange read the paper submitted by Monsieur LeBlanc, he was so impressed with its originality that he decided to track down the author. To his astonishment, he found that his star pupil was actually a young woman.

Germain's ruse was exposed. But far from being angry, Lagrange expressed his admiration and offered the young woman encouragement. Sophie Germain had found her first mathematics mentor.

A more impressive mentor would have been hard to find. Joseph-Louis Lagrange is widely regarded as one of the greatest mathematicians of the eighteenth century. The Italian-born Lagrange had planned to become a lawyer. However, his family suffered financial hardships after his father lost a considerable amount of money through bad investments. "If I had been rich," Lagrange wrote in a letter, "I probably would not have devoted myself to mathematics."

Lagrange, like Germain, taught himself the basics of mathematics. But unlike her, he went on to study under experts and to develop his skills at a university. He published his first original research under an assumed name, Luigi De la Grange Tournier, and at the young age of nineteen he received his first appointment as a professor of mathematics.

Lagrange championed a new mathematical tool, the calculus of variations, which built on the tools of calculus developed by Euler, Newton, and Gottfried Wilhelm von Leibniz. It uses derivatives and integrals to determine the set of numbers, such as a line segment or part of a curve, where a given function is always of the same value. Lagrange's

Joseph-Louis Lagrange *(Courtesy of Classic Image/Alamy)*

calculus of variations would prove to be very important to Sophie Germain's work.

In 1788, Lagrange applied his tools to Newton's work on physics. Physics is the science of looking at objects in motion and understanding the different forces that act on them. Lagrange's work in physics resulted in the development of Lagrangian mechanics, which continues to help physicists understand motion. Newton's approach to physics involved finding all of the forces acting on an object in motion at any given time. By contrast, Lagrange's method involved looking at all the possible paths for an object in motion, and identifying the one that minimized "action" (the change in energy occurring as an object moves from one place to another). As a way to analyze motion, Lagrangian mechanics provided a much simpler approach than did Newton's methods.

For example, to understand the motion of a rock falling down a mountainside, Newtonian mechanics would accommodate all the forces acting on the rock. Each force can have components in any of three dimensions, and the problem becomes complicated quickly. Using Lagrangian mechanics, a mathematician could calculate the difference between kinetic and potential energy to determine the course of least action. In 1948, the physicist Richard Feynman extended Lagrange's method to electrons and protons, atomic particles that form the basis of matter.

Lagrange was also accomplished in the fields of number theory and geometry, and he made great advances in understanding the behavior of waves. His greatest work, *Analytical Mechanics*, was published in 1788 and contained his first treatise on Lagrangian mechanics. The book was popular, and Germain often referred to it in her own work on number theory.

Before he arrived in Paris, Lagrange spent twenty years as the director of mathematics at the Berlin Academy. During that time, he won many prestigious prizes. In 1772, he and Leonhard Euler received the award from the Paris Académie des Sciences (Academy of Sciences) for their work on the three-body problem (calculating the gravitational interactions of three celestial objects). Lagrange again won the award in 1774 and 1780, both times for further work in celestial mechanics.

In 1787, Lagrange moved to Paris at the invitation of Louis XVI. Although the French king was overthrown within a few years, Lagrange remained a well-respected and highly honored Parisian. According to historians, his gift for teaching was unparalleled among his contemporaries.

Lagrange's discovery of Sophie Germain marked the end of her intellectual isolation. Now she was able to interact with the greatest mathematical minds of her day. However, a new set of obstacles arose, for French society did not seem to know what to do with a female mathematician. And shy Sophie Germain, likewise, did not seem to know how to move in French society.

three
Her Burning Effort

After Joseph Lagrange uncovered the true identity of "Antoine-August LeBlanc," Sophie Germain involuntarily entered the public world of academia. At first, she was little more than a novelty among Parisian social circles. Female mathematicians and scientists were almost unheard of in eighteenth-century France.

But Sophie Germain was not interested in being known as a female mathematician. She wanted only to be a good mathematician.

In many respects, her new connections in society proved a godsend in her pursuit of this goal. "The appearance of this young [mathematician] made quite a stir," her friend Guglielmo Libri noted, "and Mademoiselle Germain did not have to wait long to see scientists of superior merit coming to her; their conversations provided nourishment for her mind." The mathematician "Citizen" Cousin, who had written a textbook titled *Lessons on Differential and Integral Calculus*, "offered to place at her disposal all the resources he possessed for the practice and profession of science." Other scholars sent letters of support and invitations to help her with her studies. Through correspondence with a variety of academics, she was able to acquire important knowledge in fields ranging from mathematics and biology to literature and philosophy.

Yet because she was not permitted to study in a university, her intellectual development lacked the rigor and structure a formal curriculum could have provided. In addition, her gender ensured that she would always remain apart from the intellectual elite.

Some of her new colleagues deeply offended Germain with their patronizing attitudes. Many of these men underestimated her determination to pursue serious mathematics, or they failed to consider the possibility that she might be their intellectual equal—or superior.

One such man with whom Germain had highly unpleasant dealings was an aging astronomer named Joseph-Jérôme Lefrançais de Lalande. In 1785, Lalande had published a book titled *Astronomie des dames* (Astronomy for Women). Like other books of the time designed specifically to appeal to female readers, *Astronomie des dames*—which was successful enough to merit three reprintings—presented a complex scientific topic in simplified form. This, it was believed, was the only way women could understand the topic.

On November 3, 1797, Lalande took the liberty of paying Sophie Germain a personal visit. The meeting did not go well. In an unsolicited effort to help the twenty-one-year-old woman further her education, Lalande suggested that Germain read his book on astronomy. She replied that

Joseph-Jérôme Lefrançais de Lalande *(Courtesy of Visual Arts Library (London)/Alamy)*

she had no interest in a book written for women but had already read Laplace's more technical *Exposition du système du monde* (*The System of the World*). Lalande responded that he believed Germain "could not understand the one without the other," as he recounted in a letter of apology written to her the following day. Germain bristled at this suggestion. "It would be difficult for anyone to make me feel more the imprudence of my visit and the disapproval

of my respects than you did yesterday," Lalande wrote in
his apology.

Germain's dislike of Lalande became well known in
Parisian circles. In a dinner invitation to her, one host wrote:
"M. L[alande] will not be there, since you have not recon-
ciled yourself with him."

Much to Germain's chagrin, a famous scholar of ancient
Greece, Jean-Baptiste Gaspard d'Ansse de Villoison, made
light of her clash with Lalande in verse he composed in 1802,
in honor of Lalande's seventieth birthday:

Most boldly, she tries to enter
Our house, Gods stop her flight:
While you can, rein in this Icarian girl;
For her burning effort will conquer giants.
This ambitious woman already wanders in Laplace's realm! . . .

While the passage clearly was complimentary, Germain
was outraged. She wrote to Villoison and asked him to remove
from the poem the reference to her. She did not want to be
associated with Lalande in any way. Villoison complied, and
in a letter to Germain, he apologized for "shock[ing] your
modesty, which is as extraordinary as your talents."

Despite mortifying episodes such as her well-publicized
confrontation with Lalande, Sophie Germain enjoyed fruitful
professional relationships during her early and mid-twenties.
Her relationship with Lagrange continued to build, and she
began to correspond with Adrien-Marie Legendre, another
pioneer in the field of mathematical physics. Legendre, like
Laplace, had made considerable progress in the study of partial
differential equations. In the ensuing years he would become
one of Germain's most powerful mathematical allies.

However, no one exerted a greater influence on Germain's career during this period than a young German mathematician. His 1801 book affected the course of her life almost as profoundly as the biography of Archimedes she had read as a child. The young man would become one of Germain's most beloved correspondents, and she would ensure that he did not suffer the same fate as the legendary mathematician from ancient Syracuse.

four

Protecting a Kindred Spirit

During the summer of 1801, a young German mathematician named Carl Friedrich Gauss published a book titled *Disquisitiones Arithmeticae* (Arithmetical Investigations). The book's dense style and startlingly original ideas made it inaccessible to many mathematicians working at the turn of the nineteenth century. Some dismissed it as unreadable.

When Sophie Germain picked up *Disquisitiones*, however, she was electrified. Most of the book dealt with a subject that had earlier fascinated Germain and that had been addressed in works she had read by Euler and Lagrange: the often exquisitely complicated relationships among integers. But *Disquisitiones* was a systematic treatment of this abstract subject, "which in one stroke made number theory a firmly grounded and coherent part of mathematics." Germain was among the first people to recognize the significance of

Disquisitiones, and she became an early and enthusiastic proponent of its author.

History would validate her judgment. Considered one of the most important mathematics texts ever produced, *Disquisitiones Arithmeticae* stands alongside Euclid's *Elements* and Diophantus's *Arithmetica* in its influence. Its author, Carl Friedrich Gauss, is widely regarded as one of the greatest mathematicians in history.

Gauss was born in April 1777 to uneducated, working-class parents from Brunswick (a small state located in present-day Germany). His remarkable gift for mathematics was evident from an early age. With financial support from the duke of Brunswick, he was able to obtain an education. By the time Gauss enrolled in the University of Göttingen at age eighteen, his knowledge of mathematics reportedly exceeded that of many of his professors. Gauss dropped out of Göttingen but in 1799 earned a degree from the university in Brunswick. Continued financial support from the duke of Brunswick enabled him, two years later, to publish *Disquisitiones Arithmeticae*. He was only twenty-four.

Besides transforming the field of number theory in *Disquisitiones*, Gauss also proved a statement that has become known as the fundamental theorem of arithmetic: Every natural number larger than 1 can be written as the product · of prime numbers in only one way (except for the order of the factors). In other words, there is just one way to express a number as the product of its prime divisors. The number 100, for example, can be written *only* as 5 x 5 x 2 x 2.

Disquisitiones also introduced modular arithmetic, a tool that Sophie Germain would call upon in her later work. Modular arithmetic simplifies the operation of ordinary

Carl Friedrich Gauss

division and allows for complex calculations to be carried out quickly.

Gauss's book inspired Germain to begin working in earnest on problems in number theory. She studied *Disquisitiones* closely and intensely, month after month. Its ideas led her in many new mathematical directions.

In 1804, her single-minded determination to learn more about mathematics finally spurred Germain to write to Carl Friedrich Gauss. Though she was a year older than Gauss and had by this time become a formidable mathematician in her own right, she was still not confident enough to reveal her identity—including her gender—to the brilliant German. Instead she used her old pseudonym, Antoine LeBlanc. "For a long time," she wrote in her letter to Gauss, "your *Disquisitiones Arithmeticae* has been an object of my admiration and study. . . . Nothing equals the impatience with which I await the sequel to this book I hold in my hands. I have been told that you are working on it at this moment; I would spare nothing in order to procure it as soon as it appears."

But her purpose in writing was more than simply to compliment Gauss. She had tackled some of the problems he posed in his book, and she wanted his assessment on her work. "I take the liberty," she wrote, "of submitting these attempts to your judgment, persuaded that you would not demur from enlightening with your advice an enthusiastic amateur of the science you cultivate with such brilliant success."

For his part, Gauss responded enthusiastically to his new correspondent, who—unlike much of the mathematical community—had seen merit and truth in his work. He wrote back to "Antoine LeBlanc" six months later. "I read with pleasure the things you chose to communicate; it pleases me that arithmetic has acquired in you so able a friend," Gauss said. "Your new proof concerning the prime numbers for which 2 is a residue or nonresidue especially pleased me. It is very fine, although it seems to be an isolated case, inapplicable to other numbers."

The "new proof" to which Gauss referred was an analytical demonstration of a relationship—exposed through division—between certain kinds of prime numbers. Germain had included the demonstration in her letter. Gauss was quite impressed by the work of his new correspondent. He wrote to his friend and colleague, the astronomer Heinrich Olbers, "Recently I have had the joy of receiving a letter from a young Parisian mathematician, LeBlanc, who is familiarizing himself enthusiastically with higher arithmetic, and gives proofs that he has penetrated deeply into my D.A. [*Disquisitiones Arithmeticae*]."

Over the following months and years, Gauss and Germain—two kindred spirits—exchanged many letters. In the process, Gauss became one of Germain's most beloved colleagues, though she steadfastly maintained the pretense that she was Monsieur LeBlanc. In fact, her groundbreaking work on number theory, which first appeared in her letters to Gauss, might forever have been attributed to LeBlanc were it not for events set in motion by Napoleon Bonaparte.

Napoleon, one of history's most famous generals, had crowned himself emperor of France in 1804. And his territorial ambitions resulted in many years of costly wars with other European powers.

In 1806, Napoleon moved against the German states of central Europe. When Sophie Germain learned that Napoleon's forces had taken control of Brunswick, where Carl Gauss was living, she became concerned for his safety. She happened to have a friend, Joseph-Marie Pernety, who was a general in Napoleon's army. She wrote to Pernety and implored him to guarantee Gauss's safety.

Pernety complied. He sent one of his artillery officers to Brunswick to check on the German mathematician. The general soon sent a letter reassuring Germain that "this rival of Archimedes" was indeed unharmed. Pernety included the communication his artillery officer had sent to him upon finding Gauss. It was dated November 27, 1806.

Napoleon Bonaparte *(Courtesy of Classic Image/Alamy)*

Gauss, on being informed that the artillery officer had been dispatched by General Pernety on behalf of Sophie Germain, "replied that he did not have the honor of knowing" either person.

"After I had spoken of the different points contained in your orders," the artillery officer reported to Pernety, "he seemed a little confused and asked me to convey his thanks for your consideration on his behalf."

Sophie Germain decided to clear up Gauss's confusion. On February 20, 1807, she wrote to the German mathematician. "In describing the honorable mission I charged him with," she said, "M. Pernety informed me that he had made known to you my name. This has led me to confess that I am not as completely unknown to you as you might believe, but that fearing the ridicule attached to a female scientist, I have previously taken the name of M. LeBlanc in communicating to you those notes that, no doubt, do not deserve the indulgence with which you have responded."

She said she hoped that "the information that I have today confided to you will not deprive me of the honor you have accorded me under a borrowed name, and that you will devote a few minutes to write me news of yourself." She signed the letter "Your very humble servant, Sophie Germain."

Gauss was astonished to learn the identity of his longtime correspondent. He wrote to his friend Olbers: "That LeBlanc is a mere assumed name of a young lady, Sophie Germain, certainly amazes me as much as it does you."

On April 30, 1808, shortly after receiving Germain's letter, Gauss composed a long and thoughtful response. Clearly, he could not have been more delighted to find that two distant figures in his life, his correspondent LeBlanc and his French patron Sophie Germain, were in fact the same person.

He wrote to Germain:

> How can I describe my astonishment and admiration on seeing my esteemed correspondent M. LeBlanc metamorphosed into this celebrated person, yielding a copy so brilliant it is hard to believe? The taste for the abstract sciences in general and,

above all, for the mysteries of numbers, is very rare: this is not surprising, since the charms of this sublime science in all their beauty reveal themselves only to those who have the courage to fathom them. But when a woman, because of her sex, our customs and prejudices, encounters infinitely more obstacles than men in familiarizing herself with their knotty problems, yet overcomes these fetters and penetrates that which is most hidden, she doubtless has the most noble courage, extraordinary talent, and superior genius.

Gauss made clear to Germain how much he valued their correspondence. "The scientific notes with which your letters are so richly filled have given me a thousand pleasures," he revealed. "I have studied them with attention, and I admire the ease with which you penetrate all branches of arithmetic, and the wisdom with which you generalize and perfect."

Gauss went on to address some mathematical statements Germain had included with her own letter, and he pointed out a few places where her observations had been in error. He then wrote about his own work. In this way, he maintained a sort of mathematical dialogue with Germain. In his letter he included three new mathematical theorems (in mathematics, theorems are statements that have been proven analytically). Gauss did not enclose the proofs, however, "in order not to deprive you of the pleasure of finding them yourself, if you find it worthy of your time."

Shortly after writing this letter to Germain, Gauss wrote again to his friend Olbers. Germain's inspiration, he said, had led him to a new mathematical idea. "Recently I replied to a letter of hers and shared some Arithmetic with her, and this led me to undertake an inquiry again; only two days later I made a very pleasant discovery. It is a new, very neat, and short proof of the fundamental theorem of [article] 131."

Sophie Germain and Carl Gauss exchanged a few more letters, in which they discussed mathematical ideas and new approaches to the analysis of numbers. In a letter dated January 19, 1808, Gauss wrote, "Remain always happy, my dear friend. The rare qualities of your heart and mind deserve it, and continue from time to time to renew the gentle assurance that I may count myself among your friends, a title of which I will always be proud."

This turned out to be Gauss's last letter to Germain. Although she wrote to him several more times, he never again responded. Gauss received a prestigious university appointment in Göttingen, Germany, and his interests soon took him away from number theory and into a wide variety of academic disciplines, including magnetism and astronomy.

"I do not pretend to fathom the profundity of your research," Germain wrote in an 1809 letter to Gauss. "I sense that my intellect is far removed from yours, although our tasks are similar, since I, as you, have a great predilection for arithmetic problems. I find this part of science susceptible to a particular kind of elegance, which is not attained in the mathematical-physical sciences." For Germain, ideas were of intense interest in their own right, apart from any practical application they might eventually lead to. "This is not surprising," she observed, "when we consider that the human intellect, when working for its own satisfaction, should encounter the greatest intellectual beauties rather than when guided by an external motive."

Although her intellectual journey ultimately led in a different direction from that of Carl Friedrich Gauss, Sophie

Germain benefited from her correspondence with the German mathematician. The exchange of creative mathematical ideas inspired her, later in life, to return to big problems in number theory.

After Gauss had abruptly cut off their correspondence, Germain once again turned her focus closer to home. She found herself surrounded by mathematicians, including her friends and mentors Lagrange and Legendre, who were deeply concerned with the burgeoning field of mathematical physics, and she too began research in that area. Although she had matured considerably in the years since secretly obtaining course notes from the École Polytechnique, Germain was still very much a novice in research. She needed an opportunity to establish herself as a mathematician capable of deep analysis and creative insight.

Such an opportunity emerged in 1809, thanks to the emperor Napoleon, France's National Institute of Sciences and Arts, and beautiful geometric patterns that eluded scientific explanation. Germain, thirty-three years old, embarked on a project that would consume six years of her life—and eventually lead to her greatest acclaim.

Carl Gauss, Child Prodigy

Carl Friedrich Gauss made contributions to diverse areas of science, including astronomy, magnetism, and the study of electricity. But Gauss is known first and foremost as a mathematician, and his extraordinary ability with numbers was evident from early childhood.

When he was three years old, Gauss was present when his father was calculating the wages to pay his workers. The child found an arithmetic error in his father's calculations. As an elementary school student, Gauss was in a class taught by a stern instructor named J. G. Büttner. One day Büttner— who was in the habit of whipping students for incorrect answers to his questions—gave his class a computation assignment. He told them to add together all the whole numbers from 1 to 100. While the other children busied themselves with the tedious arithmetic, the young Gauss quickly calculated the answer and gave his chalk tablet to Büttner. His tablet did not show how he had arrived at his answer, but it was the correct number: 5050.

When asked to explain, Gauss said that he had simply noticed that 1 + 100 = 101, and 2 + 99 = 101, and 3 + 98 = 101. He then observed that there are 50 of these smaller sums, with the last being 50 + 51 = 101. Thus, the sum of all the numbers must be equal to 50 multiplied by 101, or 5050.

Büttner was understandably impressed and immediately ordered a better math book for the young boy. Though Gauss's working-class family demonstrated no similar talents for mathematics, Gauss proved to be amazingly gifted. By the time he was a teenager, his genius for mathematics had become well known throughout the German-speaking states of Europe.

five

Visible Music

Sophie Germain, like other mathematicians of her time, sought the answer to a compelling question: how can mathematics be used to explain scientifically the workings of the world? More specifically, how can a set of mathematical equations describe a natural phenomenon? Many mathematicians believe that, with rigorous analysis and sufficient attention to detail, systems of equations can be formulated to describe any naturally observed occurrence, from falling rain to the motion of the planets. The effort to explain one curious phenomenon would provide Germain with the opportunity to demonstrate her mathematical skills.

As her interest turned from the relationships among numbers to the application of mathematics to the real world, Germain moved quickly between two different approaches to mathematics. "Pure" mathematics, which includes number theory and the kinds of problems Germain had exchanged with Carl Gauss, involves highly abstract ideas and concepts that are only symbolically represented in the natural world. "Applied" mathematics, on the other hand, deals very explicitly with the natural world. Its practitioners seek to formulate systems of equations that will mathematically describe any observable phenomenon.

In early-nineteenth-century Paris, only a few mathematicians were concerned exclusively with concepts in pure mathematics, such as number theory. Instead, most concentrated their efforts on using mathematics to analytically describe nature. For her part, Germain tended to associate with mathematicians who could move fluidly between the two approaches.

In 1808, a German physicist named Ernst F. F. Chladni traveled to Paris, where he performed an unusual demonstration using glass plates of various shapes, a violin bow, and handfuls of sand. Because she was a woman, Germain probably did not attend his presentation for the École Polytechnique or France's National Institute of Sciences and Arts. Nevertheless, she probably did attend one of the public demonstrations he gave outside of these institutions. In addition, she was acquainted with enough members of the National Institute to get firsthand descriptions of Chladni's work.

An amateur musician, Chladni began his demonstration by sprinkling sand on the surface of the plate; he then held the plate at its edges, using a few fingers. He used the violin bow to "play" the edge of the glass plate as if it were a violin string. The plate vibrated and, in successful cases, produced a pure musical note. The vibrations jostled the grains of sand, which then began to move around on the plate. What

A pattern created by vibrating sand on a plate. *(Courtesy of sciencephotos/Alamy)*

Chladni had noticed, and what he showed his audiences in these demonstrations, was that although the movements of the sand appeared random, the tiny granules eventually lined up and formed complicated patterns.

Chladni exhibited a large number of designs, all of which were defined by straight and curved lines that intersected with each other. The points on the plate's edge where he held the plate by his fingertips always marked the beginning or end of a line. These lines represented places on the plate that were not vibrating, or nodes. The grains of sand moved around on the plate until they settled on nodes.

Ernst F. F. Chladni *(Courtesy of The Print Collector/Alamy)*

Chladni could alter the geometric patterns by changing the bow's position. He could also produce a different pattern if he held the plate with two fingers instead of three, or held the plate directly opposite the bow, perpendicular to the bow, or at some other position. The number of possible patterns seemed uncountable. Yet Chladni could always replicate a particular pattern by repeating the conditions under which it had earlier been produced. This showed that the strange shapes in the sand were not the result of random fluctuations. Instead, it seemed that every configuration of fingers, notes, and bow followed strict, invisible rules that dictated a specific pattern.

Chladni's demonstrations showcased an unexplained natural phenomenon and raised a number of interesting questions for the scientific community. Why did some parts of a plate remain motionless? Why did particular sounds result in particular patterns, and how could this relationship be demonstrated mathematically? And what did these strange new geometries—this visible music—have to do with the sounds people heard in their ears? Applied mathematics seemed to offer the possibility of answers to these questions.

Chladni's demonstrations intrigued Sophie Germain and other mathematicians and scientists in Paris. They also caught the attention of Napoleon Bonaparte. After seeing Chladni's presentation, the French emperor suggested that the First Class of the Institute—France's most prestigious scientific society— offer a prize to anyone who could develop a mathematical theory explaining the vibration of elastic surfaces.

France's scientific societies had a long tradition of sponsoring such competitions. In the 1720s the Academy of Sciences began awarding prizes for solutions to specific problems in math and science. Because the competitions were open to foreigners, and because winners enjoyed considerable acclaim in addition to receiving a monetary award, some of the best minds in Europe participated. Among the early winners was Leonhard Euler, the Swiss mathematician whose work Sophie Germain had read as a child.

In 1793, in the midst of the French Revolution, the Academy was abolished because of its ties to the toppled monarchy. But another scholarly organization, the National Institute of Sciences and Arts, was set up two years later. The First Class of the Institute, which included sixty of France's most eminent scientists, became the center of scientific inquiry in France. It reviewed current research, organized scientific expeditions, and continued in the Academy's old role of sponsoring scientific competitions.

In April 1809, the First Class of the Institute announced a *prix extraordinaire*, or grand prize, that related directly to the demonstrations of Ernst Chladni:

> His Majesty the Emperor and King, who has deigned to call M. Chladni before him and see his experiments, being struck by the impact that the discovery of a rigorous theory explaining all phenomena rendered sensible by these experiments would have on the progress of physics and analysis, desires that the Class make this the subject of a prize that will be proposed to all the learned men of Europe. . . .
>
> The class has thus proposed, for the subject of the prize, the development of a mathematical theory of the vibration of elastic surfaces, and a comparison of this theory with experiments. The prize will be a medal of gold, valued at 3000 francs. It will be awarded at a public session the first Monday of January, 1812.

Napoleon's interest in the subject was probably sufficient to ensure that Chladni's work would form the basis for the Institute's 1809 *prix extraordinaire* competition. But the emperor was likely influenced by two leading members of the First Class: Laplace and Lagrange. Pierre-Simon de Laplace, who had introduced Chladni to Napoleon, may have been the most influential member of the First Class during this period. Joseph-Louis Lagrange was one of Napoleon's most trusted scientific advisers, and he sat on the evaluating board for the contest. Some historians suggest that Lagrange (and perhaps also Laplace), in promoting this *prix extraordinaire*, may have been motivated by more than a desire to advance science. Developing a mathematical theory of the vibration of elastic surfaces seemed like the kind of problem that a protégé and lifelong friend of both men seemed well equipped to solve.

Born in 1781, Siméon-Denis Poisson had shown great mathematical ability early in his life. By 1798 he had been admitted to the École Polytechnique, where he quickly attracted the attention of his professors Laplace and Lagrange. While still a student at the school, he submitted an original paper to the First Class of the Institute. After graduating in 1800, before he had turned twenty, Poisson obtained an academic appointment at the École Polytechnique. Two years later he was made a professor at the school.

Despite these and other achievements, there was a sense that Poisson had not lived up to his potential. He had failed to gain entry into the Institute of France in 1806, despite support from Laplace and Lagrange. Winning a *prix extraordinaire*, however, would greatly advance his career.

Sophie Germain, who was only slightly older than Poisson, displayed little interest in the award but was thrilled by the intellectual challenge of explaining Chladni's vibrating plates. "Seeing M. Chladni's experiments during his stay in Paris," she revealed in a letter, "excited my interest. . . . I began studying Euler's memoir on the linear case, certainly not with the intention of competing for the *prix extraordinaire* proposed by the Institute, but only desiring to come to appreciate those difficulties that the terms of the program brought to mind."

In a 1779 paper, Leonhard Euler had derived a differential equation to describe the vibrations of an elastic beam. Euler's method described a beam moving in only one spatial dimension. However, the problem that came out of Chladni's vibrating plates required that mathematicians account for the vibrations of a two-dimensional surface. Germain used Euler's approach as a model and an entry point for analysis: it worked for one dimension, and it might work for two.

In his work, Euler had considered only small, vertical movements of the beam; he assumed that the beam did not move back and forth (in a horizontal direction). In the methods that most interested Germain, Euler explored a beam that was fixed at one or both ends, and fixed at the center of the beam. These points would define nodes (that is, points that do not move). On Chladni's plates, the unmoving nodes assumed the shape of lines.

Germain knew she had to expand Euler's work. First, she relaxed his assumption that the beam would be fixed only at the midpoint. She allowed any point along the beam to be likewise fixed. In this way, her analysis of a one-dimensional beam would be more thorough than even Euler's; it would also allow a deeper extension to two dimensions.

Second, she knew she had to expand Euler's original differential equation into another dimension. This meant incorporating sophisticated mathematical tools that she had never used before. (In particular, the analysis required that a mathematician correctly use Lagrange's calculus of variations.) For a year and a half, Germain worked diligently on the problem. Since she had no job, was supported by her father, and never moved out of the family house, she could devote herself entirely to mathematics. But some of the mathematical tools necessary to solve the problem of vibrating plates were beyond her knowledge.

In the previous few years, she had made the acquaintance of a number of France's leading intellectuals. As she worked on this problem, she often called upon a new mentor, Adrien-Marie Legendre, for assistance. Legendre was a member of the First Class of the Institute, and his work at this time contributed significantly to the development of mathematical physics. Legendre had shown his prowess as a mathematician by describing the physical motion of cannonballs. He also made significant contributions to number theory and published a leading textbook on geometry.

For nearly a year and a half, Germain and Legendre wrote back and forth. She sent him her latest ideas concerning the problem, and he responded with comments. (Even though she was well known throughout Paris, Germain communicated with her colleagues mostly through letters; personal meetings still required extensive advance planning.) Legendre objected to some of Germain's conclusions and analyses, and while much of his criticism was merited, she was able to defend her own calculations. She even identified at least one error in the analysis of the great Euler.

In one letter from early in their correspondence, which contained a rigorous exploration of Germain's work, Legendre wrote, "This result completely reconciles the theory that Mlle. Sophie wishes to adopt, despite Euler's equations and despite my first note." Legendre was clearly very interested

Adrien-Marie Legendre corresponded regularly with Germain as she attempted to solve the problem posed by Chladni's vibrating plates. *(Courtesy of Classic Image/Alamy)*

in seeing Germain succeed. He ended his letter, "Believing, Mademoiselle, that you should not be made to wait until Monday for these explanations, I send them to you as a proof of my zeal and devotion."

Shortly after she received this letter, Germain began to put her thoughts into an organized form. Her correspondence with Legendre had given her a solid base from which to attack the problem, and Euler provided a worthy model for her to emulate. For eight months, she toiled alone to write a coherent explanation of why the nodes appeared on Chladni's plates.

On September 21, 1811, a month before the contest closed, Sophie Germain submitted her work to the First Class of the Institute. By the rules of the contest, applicants did not write their name on their paper. Rather, they wrote a quotation on the front of the paper. Elsewhere, in a sealed envelope, they wrote the same quotation and their name, so that in case a paper was selected for the prize, the author could be identified.

On the front of her paper, Germain wrote the following quotation, in Latin, by Isaac Newton: "*Effectuum naturalium ejusdem generic eaedem sunt causae.*" It translates to, "Of natural effects of the same kind the causes are the same."

A month later, on October 22, Legendre wrote to Germain, who had expressed concern about the state of her paper. His note contained a startling revelation. "Your memoir," Legendre informed Germain, "is not lost; it is the only one we have received concerning the problem of the vibration of surfaces."

Not only had Germain come up with an approach to the problem; she was also the only entrant in the contest. Of all the other mathematicians working at that time, including Poisson, only she had tried her hand at the problem. But that did not imply that she would win. The committee, which included her friend Legendre, would have to scrutinize her paper line by line, equation by equation, looking for mistakes. The prizes were not given lightly, and it would be some months before the committee would finish its evaluation of Germain's work.

Ernst Chladni

When he arrived in Paris in 1808, Ernst F. F. Chladni was already a familiar figure among European intellectual circles. His first book, published in 1787, had detailed his attempts to understand how sound moves through space and to measure the speed of sound through various gases. He had subsequently become well known for his efforts to use mathematical equations to describe musical patterns. Today some historians even refer to him as "the Father of Acoustics."

Some also consider Chladni the founder of meteoritics (the study of meteorites). In 1794 he published a pioneering book on the subject, in which he correctly concluded that fireballs eyewitnesses had seen in the sky were produced by chunks of rock falling to the earth and being superheated by friction with the air. Chladni recognized that these rocks could not have been ejected from the earth by volcanic eruptions, because gravity could not explain the rocks' extremely high velocities. Chladni's conclusion that the rocks must have come from space was controversial, as it was widely believed at the time that space was empty except for the planets, stars, and comets.

six
Vibrating Plates

Joseph-Louis Lagrange famously remarked that the problem of Chladni's vibrating plates required "a new kind of analysis." Perhaps this extremely high degree of difficulty intimidated the mathematicians of the time. Other than Sophie Germain, no one—not even Siméon-Denis Poisson, Laplace's protégé—managed to submit an entry for the *prix extraordinaire*.

As she awaited news of the committee's decision regarding her paper, Germain's mentor Legendre kept her apprised of progress. Despite being the only entrant in the contest, she continued to work on the problem. She sent Legendre a letter containing an addition to her original paper, hoping that the mathematician would add it to her manuscript.

On November 10, 1811, Legendre sent a reply to Germain. "Your memoir is being circulated. . . . I will add to it the supplement," he promised. "The commissioners will then judge whether

Siméon-Denis Poisson

to take account of this supplement or not. . . . I will see to it that M. Lagrange does not delay in reading the whole thing."

As 1811 came to a close, the committee evaluated Germain's analytical description of Chladni's vibrating plates. In December, Legendre informed Germain of the progress of their work. "Mademoiselle, I do not have good news to give you concerning the examination of your memoir," he wrote. "Your principal equation is not correct, even assuming the hypothesis. . . . Your error seems to arise from the manner with which you tried to deduce the equation of a vibrating surface from the equation of a simple lamina: you became confused with the double integrals. They are nowhere amenable to the substitutions you have made. . . . There are also various other difficulties which have not yet been clarified."

The committee's decision was clear: Germain had not sufficiently explained the phenomenon. The judges did not argue with her hypothesis, which was that the elastic force of the plate is proportional to its curvature. But they did point out many mistakes in her approach and, even worse, exposed deficiencies in her mathematical abilities. In moving from hypothesis to differential equation, Germain had failed to successfully employ Lagrange's calculus of variations. In addition, she had not properly explained the equation at the heart of her paper. These shortcomings in Germain's work are in part attributable to the fact that she had taught herself the necessary mathematics rather than learning them from an expert. But her unusual education also gave her the creativity and self-reliance required to develop her hypothesis, which was the strongest part of her paper.

In his formal evaluation of her work, Lagrange presented the equation that she would have derived, had she correctly employed rigorous mathematics to her hypothesis. Lagrange arrived at this equation—which would greatly move forward the theory of vibrating surfaces and which is today recognized as correct—through Germain's highly original paper.

In December, Germain responded to Legendre. "I am not so surprised by the results you have informed me of since I had little confidence in my work," she confessed. "I was carried away by an analogy that seemed striking, but which I was not fully able to comprehend. I am most obliged to you for the care that you have taken to obtain a judgment for me and for enlightening me on the errors that I have made."

But the committee's rejection of her work did not deter Germain. Instead it seemed to inspire her to redouble her efforts. "You have revealed to me a blemish in my work," she wrote. "I felt little prepared for this and since I have deceived myself to such an extent, to the same extent I am justified in distrusting my abilities. However, I like to arrive at the truth in order to remain certain of knowledge, even when it is not favorable to me."

After judging Germain's entry insufficient, the First Class of the Institute announced that because the problem of vibrating plates remained unsolved, the next *prix extraordinaire* would be a continuation of the previous one. The deadline was extended for two years, until October 1813.

Germain returned to her manuscript. She had already dedicated two years of her life to the problem, without success. The extension of the contest gave her extra time to correct the two principal problems of her first attempt: namely, to find the correct equation with her hypothesis, and to justify the leap from hypothesis to equation. Although Lagrange had already found a suitable equation, even he could not find a satisfactory explanation for why curvature should affect the vibrations.

During this time, the young mathematician Poisson rose to prominence. In 1812, Poisson was elected to the physics division of the First Class, even though most of his significant work was in mathematics. Some historians believe that Lagrange played a key role in helping his protégé and friend gain admittance into the illustrious group. For years to come, Poisson's influence on the First Class of the Institute would prove to be a thorn in Germain's side. Yet in the short run, Poisson's election to the First Class was good news for Germain, as her greatest potential rival was now ineligible to compete for the *prix extraordinaire.*

In her second competition entry, Germain attacked the problem of Chladni's vibrating plates from a markedly different angle. Legendre had suggested in his comments that she did fully understand how to use double integrals. In calculus, an integral is a tool that allows a mathematician to sum up many continuous values over an area. For example, an integral could be used to sum up all the different masses along an elastic beam. In order to sum up all the masses over an area, a mathematician would need to use a double integral: one for length, and another for width. (And for a thick, vibrating elastic plate, a triple integral would be necessary, with the third integral accommodating the depth of the plate.)

As Germain continued working on the problem of Chladni's plates, she received some sad news. In April 1813, Joseph-Louis Lagrange, her first mathematical mentor, died at the age of seventy-seven.

By September 1813, when Germain submitted her revised work to the committee, her dense manuscript had reached a length of more than a hundred pages. Again, Germain's was the only entry for the *prix extraordinaire.*

This time she was confident in her work. "I have faith in the soundness of the theory. . . . I have examined it many times," Germain wrote in 1813. "I have compared it to the results of M. Chladni's experiments."

The committee, however, did not share Germain's positive view. Though she had been able to navigate the sophisticated mathematics required to tackle the problem, the judges did not believe she had adequately explained Chladni's plates. In December, Legendre sent her a particularly negative response: "I do not understand the analysis you send me at all; there is certainly an error in the writing or the reasoning, and I am led to believe that you do not have a very clear idea of the operations on double integrals in the calculus of variations. . . . There is a great lack of clarity in all of this."

Not all was lost, however. "It seems to be recognized," Legendre continued, "that your equation is truly that of the vibrating surface. Putting the analysis aside, the rest, concerning the explanation of the phenomena, may be good."

The committee must have agreed with Legendre's evaluation. For the great progress she had made in explaining the vibrations of elastic plates, Germain was awarded an honorable mention. This was no small feat, as the committee did not give awards simply for dedicated effort.

In 1813 the committee reopened the competition for a third and final time. The deadline for entries was October 1, 1815.

As she pursued a solution to the problem of vibrating plates, Germain discovered that scientific research was not free from political maneuvering and dishonesty. While she often remarked that it was not important who first arrived at an idea, she would feel the sting of someone else appropriating her work without crediting her. The culprit was Poisson, who commanded the respect of his fellow mathematicians by virtue of his position in the First Class of the Institute.

In August 1814, Poisson presented a paper to the Institute that included the equation Lagrange had derived from Germain's paper. Yet he made no mention of Germain's work. "Mechanics still presents several important problems that have not yet yielded to calculation; the theory of elastic surfaces, which I propose to consider in this memoir, offers a remarkable example," Poisson wrote. "The differential equations of these surfaces in static equilibrium, and more importantly, those of their movement, are not yet known."

After being appointed to the First Class in 1813, Poisson sat on the committee that evaluated Germain's work. He knew that she had won the honorable mention of the *prix extraordinaire* for her work on the very equations that, he now claimed, remained unknown. Minutes from the meeting show that Legendre objected, but Poisson presented the research as though it were his own.

Poisson, who had been in academic institutions his whole career, argued for the acceptance of Lagrange's equation based on the "corpuscular hypothesis." Championed by Laplace and enjoying wide support in the scientific community, the corpuscular hypothesis held that all matter is made up of microscopic, indivisible particles, or corpuscles, and that all natural forces act on objects in a manner similar to gravity. In the latter part of the seventeenth century, Isaac Newton had formulated an equation that accurately described the effect of gravity on two objects. Over the ensuing decades, scientists had sought to explain a broad range of physical and chemical phenomena in a similar fashion.

Newton's equation demanded that the two objects be treated as a single mass; likewise, Laplace argued, every force in nature must influence motion, first and foremost, on a molecular level. But this assumption was flawed: while elastic plates are composed of molecules, the forces that cause them to vibrate do not necessarily act according to this "corpuscular" model. Nevertheless, the assumption would hamper the science for decades to come because the corpuscular hypothesis was so widely accepted among trained scientists. Yet Sophie Germain, who had not received university training and hence was not constrained by the corpuscular hypothesis, worked toward another, more feasible explanation.

After Poisson's controversial presentation, the *prix extraordinaire* remained open. Germain attacked the problem anew, this time changing her hypothesis. Rather than trying to specifically connect the elastic force to the curvature of the plate, she simplified her work by arguing at the outset that the elastic force was connected to the ways in which the plate was deformed. In addition, she included a section addressing plates that were initially curved (rather than flat plates that bent under the influence of outside forces); this work on curvature, some mathematicians argue, provides one of the earliest analyses of surface curvature. Her third manuscript was shorter than the second. Now, after spending more than four years of her life invested in a single problem, she had proved herself a competent and confident mathematician.

For the third time, Germain's was the only entry. The committee retreated with her manuscript and examined it carefully. Her letters indicate that, as before, she continued to think about the problem even after the competition. Finally, in late 1815, the committee reached a consensus: Sophie Germain was to receive the *prix extraordinaire*!

For the first time in history, a woman received the highest honor that the French scientific establishment could bestow on a mathematician. This was not simply a landmark for women scientists; it was also a milestone in the progress of a sophisticated mathematical theory. Still, in its statement naming Germain the winner, the committee offered a qualification: the judges did not believe that her work correctly explained *all* vibrating surfaces. They did agree, however, that she had correctly explained the vibrating surfaces that Ernst F. F. Chladni had shown them four years earlier.

In the decades to follow, the theory would continue to mature. As it turned out, the approach taken by Germain—and all mathematicians of her time—was incorrect. Even though her theory proved erroneous, Sophie Germain pointed the way toward a correct theory. Missteps like Germain's are not uncommon: the history of nearly every mathematical or scientific breakthrough is marked by false starts and incorrect theories believed to be true for many years. Science requires complicated mistakes in order to progress.

Sophie Germain was the first mathematical physicist to steer the theory of vibrating surfaces away from the popular corpuscular hypothesis. While her effort to explain the patterns produced by Ernst Chladni's demonstrations ultimately proved unsuccessful, her work did lead to Lagrange's correct equation for vibrating plates, and it spurred other scientists to tackle the problem of elastic bodies generally.

The theory of elasticity, a modern term used to describe the work Sophie Germain was doing in the early nineteenth century, has a wide variety of applications. One of these is the construction of buildings. In order to create tall structures that are safe, architects and engineers must understand how the wind and the motions of the earth will cause the buildings to move. To some degree the Eiffel Tower, Paris's most recognizable landmark, owes its durability and construction to the early work of Sophie Germain.

The theory of elasticity pioneered by Germain made building
structures like the Eiffel Tower possible.

seven

In the Realm of Pure Mathematics

T hrough dedication and hard work, and with the assistance of her professional colleagues, Sophie Germain had finally emerged as a mathematician. Her work on the theory of elasticity had brought her the *prix extraordinaire*, but that work would not prove to be her greatest contribution to mathematics. Though she is recognized as a pioneer in the theory of elasticity, in the following decades, mathematicians would derive a more accurate theory in the field. Her work on vibrating surfaces was also greatly aided by the participation of many other mathematicians: Legendre helped her with her research, Lagrange advanced her theory, and Fourier helped her gain access to professional resources (without having to assume a pseudonym).

The next *prix extraordinaire*, which was set in 1816, would lead Germain to her most important contributions

Pierre de Fermat *(Courtesy of Visual Arts Library (London)/Alamy)*

to mathematics. This contest would take the forty-year-old mathematician back to one of her first loves: number theory. More than a decade earlier, this field of mathematics had inspired the flurry of letters that passed between Germain and Carl Friedrich Gauss.

For the 1816 contest, the First Class of the Institute chose one of the most celebrated unsolved problems in mathematics: Fermat's Last Theorem. Unlike the problem of Chladni's vibrating surfaces, which comes from the area of applied mathematics, this problem resides in the more abstract field of pure mathematics.

The problem first emerged in the seventeenth century. By profession Pierre de Fermat was a lawyer, but his work in mathematics ensured his place in history. Fermat never published his own work, and during his lifetime, he often posed problems to other mathematicians without offering solutions. When he died in 1665, his son collected all of his works and prepared them for publication.

One of the books in Fermat's collection was a Latin translation of Diophantus's *Arithmetica*, which had been written 2,000 years earlier. *Arithmetica* remains an important early work on number theory and methods of solving equations. Diophantus still influences mathematics: "Diophantine" equations are algebraic statements whose answers are positive integers, and Fermat's Last Theorem involves the most famous Diophantine equation in history.

The Diophantine equation at the heart of Fermat's Last Theorem is this:

$$x^n + y^n = z^n$$

The letters x, y, z, and n in this equation each stand for a positive integer greater than 0. For example, if $n = 2$, this equation becomes the Pythagorean theorem,

$$x^2 + y^2 = z^2$$

Named for Pythagoras, a Greek mathematician who lived in the sixth century BCE, the theorem states that the sum of

Pythagoras *(Courtesy of North Wind Picture Archives/Alamy)*

the squares of the two sides of a right triangle is equal to the square of the hypotenuse. In the equation above, x and y represent the lengths of the two sides, and z represents the length of the hypotenuse. There are infinitely many triplets of numbers that satisfy this equation. For example, if $x = 3$, $y = 4$, and $z = 5$, then the equation is true: $3^2 + 4^2 = 5^2$ becomes $9 + 16 = 25$. Sets of three numbers that work in this equation are called Pythagorean triplets. Other examples are (5, 12, 13), (8, 15, 17), and (7, 24, 25).

But Fermat's Last Theorem went far beyond the Pythagorean theorem. Fermat said that his equation ($x^n + y^n = z^n$) has no solutions if n is greater than 2. For example, his Last Theorem implies that it is impossible to find positive integer values for x, y, and z such that:

$$x^3 + y^3 = z^3$$

or

$$x^4 + y^4 = z^4$$

In the margin of a page in his copy of *Arithmetica*, Fermat wrote—around 1633, historians estimate—this problem. Then, beneath the statement of his theorem, he scribbled the following in Latin: "*Cuius rei demonstrationem mirabilem sane detexi. Hanc marginis exiguitas non caperet.*" Translated: "I have a truly marvelous proof of this proposition which this margin is too narrow to contain."

So Fermat posed the problem, wrote that he had a solution, and died without revealing it. Elsewhere in his notes he suggested an approach to prove the case when $n = 4$; his method, called "infinite descent," was used later by many other mathematicians, including Gauss. But Fermat did not write down the *general* solution—that is, he did not prove it for all numbers. His son searched the rest of Fermat's papers, but the proof was nowhere to be found. The statement became known as Fermat's Last Theorem not because it was the last one that he posited, but because it was the last one that remained unproven. Fermat made a number of other contributions to number theory, but because of this theorem—and the mathematical mystery surrounding it—he became one of the most famous mathematicians in history. Many historians have wondered if Fermat actually had a proof, as he claimed. The answer will never be known.

Mathematicians first approached Fermat's problem by proving it on a case-by-case basis. The first real advancement made on Fermat's Last Theorem was by Leonhard Euler, who worked on the case when $n = 3$; he did not, however, show that Fermat's theorem was true for any value of n.

This was the state of the science when, in 1816, the First Class pronounced Fermat's Last Theorem the subject of the *prix extraordinaire*. Germain had been interested in the problem for a long time. In her letters to Gauss, written more than ten years earlier, she had begun developing her thoughts on the problem.

Germain tried to resume her correspondence with Gauss in 1819, as she worked on proving Fermat's Last Theorem. "Although I have labored for some time on the theory of vibrating surfaces, . . . I have never ceased to think of the theory of numbers," she informed the German mathematician. "I will give you an idea of my preoccupation for this kind of research in avowing to you that, even without any hope of success, I prefer it to work that necessarily gives me results. A long time before our Academy proposed as the subject of a prize the proof of the impossibility of Fermat's equation, this challenge . . . has often tormented me."

But Gauss had moved on in his studies and no longer responded to Germain's letters. After the *prix extraordinaire* was announced, a friend wrote to Gauss and suggested he work on the problem. Gauss wrote back, "I am very much obliged for your news concerning the Paris prize. But I confess that Fermat's Last Theorem as an isolated proposition has very little interest for me, for I could easily lay down a multitude of such propositions, which one could neither prove nor disprove."

Germain did not develop her own theory until she resumed her correspondence with Legendre, who had been instrumental to her success with the theory of elasticity. In her letters to both Gauss and Legendre, she noted that mathematicians had been working on a case-by-case basis, and she sought a more general approach. With Legendre's guidance, she was able to form her ideas into a coherent method for attacking Fermat's Last Theorem.

She knew that instead of eliminating cases one by one, a mathematician could actually eliminate entire classes of numbers. This was common knowledge: for example, if one could show that the theorem was true for $n = 4$ (as Fermat had), then the theorem was necessarily true for all multiples of four. For any even value of n, the equation could be written such that the exponent was 4. For example, $x^{12} + y^{12} = z^{12}$ could be rewritten as $(x^3)^4 + (y^3)^4 = (z^3)^4$.

By this method of factorization, mathematicians had recognized that Fermat's Last Theorem was true for all even numbers, and for all composite numbers. By the time Germain worked on the problem, what remained to be shown was that the theorem was true for prime numbers—that is, any integer other than 0, 1, and -1 that is divisible only by itself and 1. The numbers 2, 3, 5, and 7 are the first four prime numbers. Germain worked on the prime numbers, and her groundbreaking method would later be used by other mathematicians. She never published her work, but it did appear in the memoirs of Legendre and in other papers written later.

Germain demonstrated the following conclusion. Suppose the exponent, n, of the equation is prime, and suppose also that $2n + 1$ is prime. This group of numbers would include 5, for example, because $2(5) + 1 = 11$, and 11 is also prime. It would also include 23, a prime, because $2(23) + 1 = 47$ is also prime. The group would exclude a number like 7, because $2(7) + 1 = 15$, and 15 is not prime (it is divisible by 5 and 3); it would also exclude 13, because $2(13) + 1 = 27$, and 27 is not prime.

If the exponent of Fermat's equation is equal to one of these prime numbers, Germain showed that one of the numbers x, y, or z must be divisible by that prime number. (Mathematicians say that x, y, or z must be "coprime" with the exponent.) Thus, she simplified the process of proving Fermat's Last Theorem for a group of numbers: if the exponent does not evenly divide one of the numbers x, y, or z, then the equation cannot be solved for that exponent. And if the equation cannot be solved, then Fermat's Last Theorem holds for that prime number.

These prime numbers have come to be called Germain primes, after Sophie Germain. In addition, "Sophie Germain's Theorem" was presented by Legendre to the French Academy of Sciences in 1823; he included her work in all subsequent versions of his papers. Sophie Germain's Theorem is still used by number theorists; it provides a roadmap to proving Fermat's Last Theorem for certain groups of numbers. She used her new method to prove one case of Fermat's Last Theorem for every prime number less than 100.

Mathematicians and computer scientists still use the ideas put forth by Sophie Germain; the largest Germain prime on record has more than 51,000 digits. Prime numbers form the

Andrew John Wiles solved
Fermat's Last Theorem
in 1994. *(Courtesy of © C. J.
Mozzochi, Princeton N.J.)*

backbone of Internet security; by identifying large Sophie Germain primes, computer scientists can devise new ways to secure cyberspace.

Germain wrote, but never published, a twenty-four-page document, "Remarks on the impossibility of satisfying the equation $x^p + y^p = z^p$"; it is contained in an archive in Florence, Italy. News of her results eventually spread through the mathematical community, and in the decades following her breakthrough, Germain's methods were used by many eminent mathematicians. Again, she had tackled a difficult problem and made admirable progress. Fermat's Last Theorem outlived Germain and all of her contemporaries. In fact, it remained unproven until 1994, when British-born Andrew John Wiles, a mathematician at Princeton University, successfully proved it to be true for all numbers, using mathematical tools unimagined in the previous century.

Germain's work on Fermat's Last Theorem is an important chapter in the history of number theory, and mathematicians continue to build on and refine her methods. But during her time, Germain was respected as a mathematician only within a small circle. Her mentor Lagrange had passed away, and her accomplishments in number theory were fully appreciated only by Legendre and, after her death, by Gauss. However, the friends she did have were among the intellectual elite of the era and proved to be good resources for the rest of her career.

Diophantine Equations

Diophantus of Alexandria lived around the third century CE. His tombstone was said to be engraved with the following riddle, which describes his life mathematically (this translation is by the physicist Stephen Hawking, in *God Created the Integers*):

His boyhood lasted $1/6$ of his life.
He grew a beard after another $1/12$.
After $1/7$ more he married.
And had a son 5 years later.
The son lived to half the father's age.
And the father died 4 years later.

This problem represents a type of algebraic structure introduced by Diophantus (the solution is at the end of this sidebar).

Diophantus's most famous book, the *Arithmetica*, outlines ways to solve certain types of algebraic equations. The *Arithmetica* originally contained thirteen books, but some of them have been lost. Six of them were well known in the Western world, and in the late twentieth century, four more were discovered at the shrine of Imam Rezā in northeastern Iran.

In honor of the *Arithmetica*, equations whose solutions are positive integers have become known as "Diophantine equations." While Diophantus did use fractions in his original book, they generally do not appear in modern-day Diophantine equations.

Many professional mathematicians have made careers out of studying Diophantine equations; many have explored the question of how to determine whether or not a given equation has a solution. In the twentieth century, one of the most famous unsolved problems was the question of how to construct an algorithm that would always tell whether or not a given Diophantine equation has a solution.

Solution to Diophantus's Riddle

1. Set up two equations:

$$d = (\tfrac{1}{6} + \tfrac{1}{12} + \tfrac{1}{7})d + 5 + s + 4$$
$$s = \tfrac{1}{2}d$$

where d is the number of years Diophantus lived, and s is the number of years his son lived.

2. Substitute ½d for s in the first equation and solve according to algebraic rules.

Sophie Germain Primes

A prime number is divisible only by itself and 1. A "Sophie Germain prime," which Germain first identified in her correspondence with Gauss, is a prime number p such that 2p + 1 is also a prime number. Thus, 5 is a Sophie Germain prime because 2(5) + 1 = 11, and 11 is also prime. However, 7 is not a Sophie Germain prime because 2(7) + 1 = 15, and 15 is not prime, being divisible by 5 and 3.

For small numbers, it is relatively straightforward to test whether or not a number is prime: simply try to divide the number by all known primes that are less than half the number. The number 39, for example, is not divisible by 2, but it is divisible by 3; hence, it is not prime. On the other hand, 41 is not divisible by 2, 3, 5, 7, 11, 13, 17, or 19; hence, it is prime. This testing technique quickly becomes cumbersome with larger numbers: to test whether or not 1147 is prime, for example, requires many operations of division. (The number 1147 is, in fact, prime.)

Mathematicians and computer scientists work to develop more efficient ways to test the primality of a number. This is more than just an exercise in number theory: when information is passed over the Internet, it is encoded using the product of two very large prime numbers. Computer programmers have confidence in the encryption because it is so difficult to tell whether or not a number is prime, and which prime numbers divide a large number. If there were an easy way to factor large numbers, Internet security would be compromised.

As of May 3, 2006, the largest known Sophie Germain prime had more than 51,000 digits. It was found by Zoltán Járai, Gabor Farkas, Timea Csajbok, Janos Kasza, and Antal Járai, who wrote and implemented a computer program to find it.

eight

Closed Doors

Even with the *prix extraordinaire* to her credit, Germain had a hard time gaining the respect of the intellectual establishment in Paris. She had come a long way: her status as a serious mathematician deepened her professional and personal relationships with some of the great scientific minds of her time. Nonetheless, she was not allowed to join the Academy of Sciences (the old name was restored in 1816), much less attend lectures of the First Class of the Institute. The Academy—now an autonomous organization forming a part of the Institute—was the scientific heart of Paris, and any man who had done as much work as Germain would almost certainly have been invited to join. Participation in the Academy would have given her access to ongoing research, including research that had grown out of her own work on elastic surfaces.

An eighteenth-century lecture at the French Academy of Sciences. (*Courtesy of Mary Evans Picture Library/Alamy*)

In 1821, the permanent secretary of the Academy of Sciences was an astronomer named Jean-Baptiste-Joseph Delambre. Germain very much wanted to attend public lectures at the Institute, and she asked Delambre on more than one occasion to find an extra ticket for her. He was not particularly accommodating. "For several years now," Delambre informed Germain in a July 1821 letter, "the established order for the distribution of places at public sessions seems to me, as well as to you, susceptible to more than one objection. . . . According to a royal ordinance, however, each Academy can dispose of its places according to its own conventions. . . . [A]t each meeting of our Academy I have at most ten tickets. I make it a rule to distribute them to those of my fellow members who want them for their wives." For a scientist of Sophie Germain's caliber, being shut out of Academy lectures under such circumstances must have been difficult to bear.

But this snub was not the only difficulty Germain encountered: her professional relationship with Poisson, who was a member of the Academy, remained tense. After the committee had given her the *prix extraordinaire*, with its reservations, she had written to Poisson: "The judgment pronounced by the class taught me that I had been deceived by the proof that had been acceptable to you, but it did not explain to me the nature of the error I made. . . . I do not think I was mistaken in the manner in which the general equation was deduced from the hypothesis." She then asked Poisson for a concrete analysis of her arguments, pointing out where she had erred, but he never provided one.

From Legendre, she also heard about Poisson's work and about his failure to credit her hypothesis, and she tried to engage him in a mathematical dialogue. He responded curtly: she would have to wait for his published paper to view his argument.

Germain decided that her work on the theory of elasticity also deserved to be published. Legendre had actually suggested this after Germain's second entry in the *prix extraordinaire* competition had been awarded an honorable mention in 1814. But because the judging committee had said that her work lacked rigor, the Academy of Sciences would not publish it. Thus Germain had to publish it herself. In 1820, Legendre enlisted one of his colleagues, Jean-Baptiste-Joseph Fourier, to help Germain in this endeavor.

These were particularly tumultuous years for France. In 1814, after several years of costly military campaigns, Napoleon was finally defeated by a coalition of European allies. Foreign forces occupied Paris, Napoleon was exiled to the island of Elba, and the French monarchy was restored when Louis

Jean-Baptiste-Joseph Fourier *(Courtesy of Hulton Archive/Getty Images)*

XVIII, the younger brother of Louis XVI, was made king. But in early 1815, Napoleon escaped from Elba, returned to France, and raised a new army. He was not subdued until June, at the Battle of Waterloo. Yet internal upheaval continued in France. Following the death of Louis XVI in 1824, Charles X ascended to the throne. His attempts to restore absolute power to the monarchy provoked increasing popular opposition, and revolution again rocked France in 1830.

This was also a time of change for Germain. She continued working to establish her place as a professional mathematician among the French intellectual elite. She developed a warm friendship with Fourier, who was a member of the Academy of Sciences.

Like Germain, Fourier was unmarried, and like her he had had to surmount great obstacles to become a mathematician. As a boy, he had gone to school at a military academy run by Benedictine monks, and he had scavenged in the school's

A scene from the French Revolution of 1830 *(Courtesy of Visual Arts Library (London)/Alamy)*

cabinets to find candles in order to study through the night. Like Germain, Fourier had spent his childhood satisfying his curiosity about mathematics and developing his skills. In the mid-1790s he taught at the École Polytechnique, but in 1798 he was called away to military service, accompanying Napoleon's army to Egypt as a scientific adviser. Upon his return to France three years later, Fourier was appointed prefect of Isère, in southeastern France. While it would be more than a dozen years before he returned to Paris, Fourier managed to conduct research while fulfilling his administrative duties in Isère. His scientific work, like Germain's, centered on applied mathematics, and he also worked on the theory of elasticity.

In the early 1820s, as Germain began to prepare her work on elastic surfaces for publication, Fourier offered her words of encouragement. "Monsieur Legendre has wished on your behalf that I undertake a study of a memoir on the properties of elastic surfaces," he wrote. "I have very attentively read this work and I have found there new proofs of the success of your research on this difficult problem." Fourier and Germain met, at her home, to exchange ideas about her theory and organize her work.

As Germain was finishing up her paper, however, Fourier was called away to tend to other duties. "I am convinced that you will have developed further the theory with which you occupy yourself, and which I invite you to publish right away," he wrote to her in a letter. "No one can treat this difficult and interesting problem with more success." In another letter, Fourier assured her that he longed "to take up again our analytical conversations, because you bring to them much intelligence and a marvelous wisdom."

But some historians suggest that Fourier was actually seeking to remove himself from Germain's publishing project because she had included in her manuscript a new, untested area of mathematical research, and he could neither vouch for its accuracy nor take the time to study it in depth. The subject was her investigation of curved surfaces, which she had first proposed in her second attempt to win the *prix extraordinaire*. Because she didn't fully understand how to use all of the necessary mathematical tools, however, Germain's analysis may have been inaccurate.

Nonetheless, she was determined to include her analysis in her manuscript. "The theory that I seek to establish," she wrote, "is not yet known to the public." Despite this resolve, Germain seems to have harbored some doubts about her work. In the preface of her manuscript, she wrote, "If sometimes I speak in an affirmative tone, it is only to free myself from the tiring expression of doubt." She also included direct references to the work of Poisson, whom she called "the geometer with whom I have the misfortune of not sharing an opinion."

Germain published her paper in 1821. It quickly drew praise from luminaries of science and mathematics, including many members of the Academy. "I have gratefully received the work which you deigned to send me," Claude-Louis Navier, who pursued a theory of elasticity for many years, informed Germain. "Reading it has inspired me with great interest, and I appreciate, equally, the value of a composition so remarkable, one that few men can read and that only a woman could write."

Delambre, who had thwarted Germain's attempts to gain entrance to the lectures of the Academy, wrote to express the group's appreciation of her work. "The Academy has received with the greatest interest the work that you have seen fit to address to us," he said. "The Academy in expressing its recognition of this new proof of your talents, has instructed me to thank you in its name for having submitted this interesting memoir, which it has had the honor of placing in the Library of the Institute."

However, such praise rang somewhat hollow. For even as eminent mathematicians wrote Germain to express their compliments, the theory of elasticity—through the work of Navier, Fourier, and others—was growing in new directions. Germain's theory was nearly obsolete by the time it appeared in published form.

Still, after garnering accolades from her peers, Germain finally won the right to do something she had long desired. In 1822, Fourier became the permanent secretary of the Academy of Sciences, and one of his first official acts was to notify Germain that she could attend the scientific lectures of the Institute of France—not as the wife or guest of a member but as a scientist in her own right. This was the first time a woman had been recognized in this manner. "I have the honor of informing you," Fourier wrote, "that every time you wish to attend the public meetings of the Institute you will be admitted to one of the reserved seats in the middle of the hall. The Academy of Sciences wishes to demonstrate, by this distinction, all the interest that your mathematical works inspire, especially the scientific research that it has crowned through the award to you of one of its annual, grand prizes."

Fourier's assurances notwithstanding, Germain reported in later letters that she still sometimes had difficulty gaining admission to lectures. She never truly felt accepted by the scientific community. "I find myself foreign to the movement of the sciences," she revealed in an especially poignant letter, "as if [I am in] another country."

nine
Daughter of Genius

For the rest of the 1820s, Sophie Germain attended as many scientific lectures as she could, and she continued to do mathematical research. Yet she worried, given her past experiences with Poisson, that her work might not receive serious treatment. She was less concerned with the credit due her than with the growth of the science; she believed she had much to offer researchers. To assuage her fears, her friend Fourier kept her informed of the Academy's proceedings and of its treatment of her work.

In 1826, Germain published another paper on her latest analyses, but this paper did not represent a mathematical advancement. Her letters from this time reflect a growing insecurity. Although permitted to attend lectures, she still could not attend classes or pursue research within the academic system. She remained an outsider to the scientific community, as she had been her entire life.

But she was a well-respected outsider: as the theory of elasticity continued to advance, her contributions were often cited in other research. Navier, who had been elected to the Academy of Sciences in 1824, made a point of singling out her work as a major breakthrough. "The research [of Sophie Germain]," he said, "was founded on an ingenious hypothesis." Navier consistently credited her hypothesis with determining the correct course of mathematical research.

Germain, for her part, stood up for herself. In a note published in the *Annals of Chemistry* in 1828, she described her work on the theory of elasticity and pointed out that she had been the first mathematician to doubt the usefulness of thinking of elastic force as a molecular action.

Mathematics and the sciences, however, were not the only subjects on her mind. Throughout her life, Germain had recorded her philosophical ruminations in a journal. Sometime near the end of the 1820s, she began work on an essay that pulled together these thoughts. Germain did not get the chance to complete the essay, titled "Considerations on the State of the Sciences and of Letters at the Different Periods of Their Culture," but her nephew, Jacques-Amant Lherbette, published it two years after her death.

"Considerations" touched on a wide range of subjects, including music, literature, the history of human thought and culture, and the characteristics of society. In an especially interesting section, Germain argued that all intellectual activity—from mathematics and science to painting and poetry—begins with insight and imagination. But such inspiration alone is insufficient to produce scientific or artistic advancements; reason or the application of a rigorous method, she suggested, is also necessary. In Germain's view, the same kinds of fundamental laws that govern mathematics and the physical sciences—laws that can be discovered through observation, experimentation, and reason—also govern society and even individual ethical behavior.

Germain's ideas, several writers have asserted, deeply influenced the French philosopher Auguste Comte. Comte, who knew Germain socially and who praised her philosophical work, founded the philosophical school known as positivism. Among its key tenets was the idea that progress toward a more just political and social order, as well as greater individual morality, would come from knowledge derived from the sciences rather than from theology or metaphysics. Writing nearly fifty years after Germain's death, one historian of philosophy argued that "the Positivism which, without the use of the word, one finds in the writings of Sophie Germain, contains the essential features of that which has hitherto been associated with the name of Auguste Comte." Another philosopher called her "the predecessor of Comte."

In her later years, Germain cultivated friendships with many members of the next generation of mathematicians. Her letters show that these relationships were as personal as they were professional; Germain was always willing to offer help to younger mathematicians. The most significant of these relationships was with the Italian mathematician Guglielmo Libri.

In 1824, Libri went to Paris from Italy, where he had been a professor of mathematics at the University of Pisa. He and Sophie Germain met on May 13, 1825, at an evening party hosted by the astronomer François-Jean Arago. Libri was twenty-six years younger than Germain, but the two had much in common. In 1819, Libri, hearing of the *prix extraordinaire*

The ideas expressed in Germain's "Considerations" influenced French philosopher Auguste Comte. *(Courtesy of Mary Evans Picture Library/Alamy)*

offered by the French Academy of Sciences, had begun his own research on Fermat's Last Theorem. He established himself as a prodigy in the field of number theory—a subject close to Germain's heart. He and Germain struck up a friendship that would last the rest of her life.

Germain and Guglielmo Libri corresponded regularly, and remained close friends until Germain's death in 1831.

Libri stayed in Paris only about three months, but during that time he and Germain met on several occasions. An avid historian of mathematics, Libri enlisted her help in obtaining archival manuscripts from the French Academy. Over the next four years, Germain and Libri corresponded regularly. While many of their letters have been lost, the correspondence that remains attests to the closeness of their friendship.

In 1829, Sophie Germain was diagnosed with breast cancer. She soon became too ill to pursue her research with the same focus she had previously employed. However, she did muster enough energy and determination in 1830 to produce one last paper, which appeared in a Berlin journal that year. The paper dealt with curvature, a concept that she had discussed with Gauss twenty-five years before. But it was not simply the subject of the paper that took Germain back to an earlier time in her life. Outside the walls of her home, the streets of Paris were again being shaken by revolutionary violence. The fifty-four-year-old Sophie Germain found refuge from the distressing events of July 1830 in the same way the young Sophie Germain had found refuge from the horrors of the French Revolution—by losing herself in study.

In one sense, Sophie Germain's life was one of remarkable continuity. It was a life spent in the single-minded pursuit of mathematical and scientific knowledge. Yet, as she understood, human existence—unlike the laws of science—is characterized by constant change, and it is fleeting. "Space and time: these man proposes to measure," Germain wrote in her journal. "The one circumscribes his momentary existence, the other accompanies his successive stages in life. These two dimensions are tied together through a necessary relationship, namely, motion. When motion is constant and uniform, space is known by time and time is measured by space. Man has nothing within him that is constant and uniform; continually modified every instant, he is changing, irregular, and hardly durable enough to be a measure of duration."

In the final weeks of her life, Germain wrote twice to Libri, who was facing political struggles in his native country. He had lost his citizenship and was about to be forced into exile. Her last letter, dated April 18, 1831, began with an expression of concern for Libri's well-being. "Monsieur," she wrote, "I am more afflicted than astonished by what you tell me concerning your present situation. I see you disquieted, the disposition of your spirit far removed from the exclusive love of the sciences, which would have made you happy."

Her empathy was remarkable given what she revealed next in the letter. "My health," she said, "is in a frightful state. A prompt death would be a relief to me because I suffer from unbelievable pain, which leaves me not a moment's rest."

Sophie Germain's suffering finally ended two months later. On June 27, 1831, the mathematician died at the age of fifty-five.

Libri wrote an obituary for his friend. The brief remembrance was printed in a newspaper one year after Germain's death. It emphasized not just the importance of her mathematical achievements, but also the nobility of her character:

> She rejoiced even when she saw her ideas made fruitful on occasion by other persons who adopted them. . . . She said, happily, that her ideas had produced their fruit for science while not yielding anything for her reputation—which she scorned and amusingly called the glory of the bourgeois, the small place we occupy in the mind of others.

This noble character she also displayed in her actions, actions always marked by the stamp of virtue, which she said she cherished as a mathematical truth. Since she could not conceive that one could love the ideas of one kind of order without loving those of another, the ideas of justice or virtue were, following her thinking, ideas of order that the mind ought to adopt, even when the heart did not cherish them.

Such was this superior woman, who of all who pursued mathematical studies the farthest, the only one, to our knowledge, who has made real progress. The theory of sound and indeterminate analysis will keep her name alive for a long time.

Six years after Sophie Germain's passing, the professors at the University of Göttingen—a university renowned for producing influential mathematicians—were discussing possible recipients of honorary degrees, when Carl Friedrich Gauss suggested that Sophie Germain receive a special honor. It was only then that he learned of her death.

Mathematical truths, unlike mathematicians, are eternal, and Sophie Germain's work on number theory continues to inspire modern number theorists. And her work on the theory of elasticity is now regarded as a valuable part of mathematical history, even though some aspects of scientific culture have conspired against her legacy. In his 1913 book *Women in Science*, the historian H. J. Mozans summed up this failure to adequately acknowledge Germain's achievements:

And yet, strange as it may seem, when the state official came to make out the death certificate of this eminent associate and co-worker of the most illustrious members of the French Academy of Science, he designated her as a *rentière-annuitant* [a single woman with no profession]—not as a *mathématicienne*. Nor is this all. When the Eiffel Tower was erected in which the engineers were obliged to give special attention to the elasticity of the materials used, there were inscribed on this lofty structure the names of seventy-two savants. But one will not find in this list the name of that daughter of genius, whose researches contributed so much toward establishing the theory of the elasticity of metals, Sophie Germain. Was she excluded from this list . . . because she was a woman? It would seem so. If such, indeed, was the case, more is the shame for those who were responsible for such ingratitude toward one who had deserved so well of science, and who by her achievements had won the enviable place in the hall of fame.

timeline

1776	Marie-Sophie Germain born April 1 in Paris, France.
1789	Reads J. E. Montucla's *History of Mathematics*; French Revolution begins.
1795	Begins submitting work to Lagrange and Fourcroy at the École Polytechnique, under the name of Antoine-August LeBlanc; eventually discovered by Lagrange.
1801	Reads *Disquisitiones Arithmeticae*, by Carl Friedrich Gauss.
1804	Writes letter to Gauss, using pseudonym Antoine LeBlanc.
1806	Entreats a friend, General Pernety, to ensure Gauss's safety from Napoleon's army; reveals her true identity to Gauss.
1809	Begins working on mathematical explanation of Ernst Chladni's vibrating plates.
1811	Submits explanation for the *prix extraordinaire*.
1812	Entry deemed insufficient; the contest is extended.
1813	Submits her second attempt to win *prix extraordinaire*.
1814	Second attempt still fails to satisfy the judges, but receives an honorable mention for efforts; contest is again extended.

1815 Submits third entry.

1816 Wins the *prix extraordinaire*; resumes study of number theory and Fermat's Last Theorem.

1821 Publishes work on theory of elasticity.

1822 Allowed to attend lectures at the Institute of France.

1830 Final paper, an analysis of curvature, published in Berlin.

1831 Dies of cancer in Paris.

Sources

CHAPTER ONE: Finding Inspiration

p. 13-14, "all obstacles which her family . . . ." Louis L. Bucciarelli and Nancy Dworsky, *Sophie Germain: An Essay in the History of the Theory of Elasticity* (Dordrecht, Holland: D. Reidel Publishing Company, 1980), 10.

p. 17-18, "I beg you . . ." Valerius Maximus, *Memorable Doings and Sayings,* vol. 2, book 9, trans. and ed. D. R. Shackleton Bailey (Cambridge, MA: Loeb Classical Library, Harvard University Press, 2000).

p. 18, "Mademoiselle Germain . . ." Bucciarelli and Dworsky, *Sophie Germain*, 117.

p. 20-21, "Mathematicians have tried in vain . . ." G. Simmons, *Calculus Gems* (New York: McGraw Hill, 1992), http://math.furman.edu/~mwoodard/ascquote.html.

CHAPTER TWO: Monsieur LeBlanc and Professor Lagrange

p. 29, "This forgetting of self . . ." Bucciarelli and Dworsky, *Sophie Germain*, 118.

p. 30, "If I had been rich . . ." J. J. O'Connor and E. F. Robertson, "Joseph-Louis Lagrange," MacTutor History of Mathematics archive, http://www-groups.dcs. st-and.ac.uk/~history/Biographies/Lagrange.html.

CHAPTER THREE: Her Burning Effort

p. 34, "The appearance . . ." Bucciarelli and Dworsky, *Sophie Germain*, 12.

p. 35, "offered to place . . ." Ibid.

p. 36, "could not understand the one . . ." Ibid., 13.

p. 36-37, "It would be difficult . . ." Ibid.

p. 37, "M. L[alande] will not . . ." Ibid.

p. 37, "Most boldly, she tries . . ." Ibid., 15.

p. 37, "shock[ing] your modesty . . ." Ibid., 14.

CHAPTER FOUR: Protecting a Kindred Spirit

p. 39, "which in one stroke . . ." Tord Hall, *Carl Friedrich Gauss: A Biography*, trans. Albert Froderberg (Cambridge, MA: MIT Press, 1970), 48.

p. 42, "For a long time . . ." Bucciarelli and Dworsky, *Sophie Germain*, 21.

p. 42, "I take the liberty . . ." Ibid.

p. 42, "I read with pleasure . . ." Ibid.

p. 43, "Recently I have had . . ." Ibid., 27.

p. 43, "this rival of Archimedes," Ibid., 24.

p. 44, "replied that he did not . . ." Ibid., 23.

p. 44-45, "After I had spoken . . ." Ibid.

p. 45, "In describing the honorable mission . . ." Ibid., 24.

p. 45, "the information that I . . ." Ibid., 25.

p. 45, "Your very humble servant, . . ." Ibid.

p. 45, "That LeBlanc is a mere . . ." Ibid., 28.

p. 45-46, "How can I describe . . ." Ibid., 25.

p. 46, "The scientific notes . . ." Ibid.

p. 46, "in order not to deprive . . ." Ibid., 26.

p. 46-47, "Recently I replied . . ." Ibid., 27.

p. 47, "Remain always happy . . ." Ibid.

p. 47, "I do not pretend . . ." Ibid., 121.

p. 47, "This is not surprising . . ." Ibid.

CHAPTER FIVE: Visible Music

p. 55, "His Majesty . . ." Bucciarelli and Dworsky, *Sophie Germain*, 35.

p. 56-57, "Seeing M. Chladni's experiments . . ." Ibid., 41.
p. 58, "This result completely . . ." Ibid., 50.
p. 59, "Believing, Mademoiselle . . ." Ibid.
p. 60, "Effectuum . . ." Ibid., 51.
p. 60, "Your memoir . . ." Ibid., 52.

CHAPTER SIX: Vibrating Plates
p. 62, "a new kind of analysis," Bucciarelli and
   Dworsky, *Sophie Germain*, 40.
p. 62-63, "Your memoir is being . . ." Ibid., 52.
p. 63, "Mademoiselle, I do not . . ." Ibid., 54.
p. 64, "I am not so surprised . . ." Ibid., 58.
p. 64-65, "You have revealed to me . . ." Ibid., 59.
p. 66, "I have faith . . ." Ibid., 61.
p. 66, "I do not understand . . ." Ibid., 63.
p. 67, "It seems to be recognized . . ." Ibid.
p. 67, "Mechanics still presents . . ." Ibid., 65.

CHAPTER SEVEN: In the Realm of Pure Mathematics
p. 76, "I have a truly marvelous . . ." *NOVA* Online,
   "Solving Fermat: Andrew Wiles," http://www.pbs.org/
   wgbh/nova/proof/wiles.html.
p. 77, "Although I have labored . . ." Bucciarelli and
   Dworsky, *Sophie Germain*, 86.
p. 77-78, "I am very much obliged . . ." Simon Singh,
   *Fermat's Engima: The Epic Quest to Solve the World's
   Greatest Mathematical Problem* (New York: Walker and Co.
   1977), 105.

CHAPTER EIGHT: Closed Doors
p. 85, "For several years now . . ." Bucciarelli and
   Dworsky, *Sophie Germain*, 90.
p. 86-87, "The judgment pronounced . . ." Ibid., 82.

p. 89, "Monsieur Legendre has wished . . ." Ibid., 91.

p. 89, "I am convinced . . ." Ibid.

p. 89, "to take up again . . ." Ibid., 92.

p. 90, "The theory that I seek . . ." Ibid., 93.

p. 90, "If sometimes I speak . . ." Ibid., 94.

p. 90, "the geometer with whom . . ." Ibid., 93.

p. 90, "I have gratefully . . ." Ibid., 95.

p. 91, "The Academy has received . . ." Ibid., 96.

p. 91, "I have the honor . . ." Ibid., 89.

p. 92, "I find myself foreign . . ." Andrea Del Centina, "Letters of Sophie Germain Preserved in Florence," *Historia Mathematica* 32, no. 1 (February 2005): 60-75.

CHAPTER NINE: Daughter of Genius

p. 94, "The research . . ." Bucciarelli and Dworsky, *Sophie Germain*, 103.

p. 95, "the Positivism . . ." Jesse Fernandez Martinez, "Sophie Germain," *Scientific Monthly* 63, no. 4 (October 1946): 260.

p. 95, "the predecessor of Comte," Ibid.

p. 98-99, "Space and time: . . ." Bucciarelli and Dworsky, *Sophie Germain*, 53.

p. 99, "Monsieur . . ." Ibid., 121.

p. 99, "My health . . ." Ibid.

p. 99, "She rejoiced even when . . ." Ibid., 118.

p. 100, "And yet . . ." M. Thomas a Kempis, "An Appreciation of Sophie Germain," *National Mathematics Magazine* 14, no. 2 (November 1939): 90.

Bibliography

Aczel, Amir. *Fermat's Last Theorem: Unlocking the Secret of an Ancient Mathematical Problem.* New York: Four Walls Eight Windows, 1996.

Bucciarelli, Louis, and Nancy Dworsky. *Sophie Germain: An Essay in the History of the Theory of Elasticity.* Dordrecht, Holland: D. Reidel Publishing Co., 1980.

Centina, Andrea Del. "Letters of Sophie Germain Preserved in Florence." *Historia Mathematica* 32, no. 1 (February 2005), 60–75.

Dalmedico, Amy. "Sophie Germain." *Scientific American,* December 1991, 116–120.

Dunnington, G. Waldo. *Carl Friedrich Gauss: Titan of Science.* New York: Hafner Publishing Co., 1955.

Germain, Sophie. *Remarques sur la nature, les bornes et l'etendue de la question des surfaces elastiques.* Paris: Huzard-Courcier, 1826.

———. *Memoire sur la courbure des surfaces.* Berlin: G. Reimer, 1830.

Hall, Tord. *Carl Friedrich Gauss: A Biography.* Translated by Albert Froderberg. Cambridge, MA: MIT Press, 1970.

Hawking, Stephen, ed. *God Created the Integers: The Mathematical Breakthroughs That Changed History.* Philadelphia: Running Press, 2005.

Libri, G. "Notice sur Mlle Sophie Germain." *Journal des Débats,* May 18, 1832.

Martinez, Jesse A. Fernandez. "Sophie Germain," *Scientific Monthly* 63, no. 4 (1947), 257-260.

Mozans, H. J. *Woman in Science.* South Bend, IN: University of Notre Dame Press, 1991.

Osen, Lynn M. *Women in Mathematics.* Cambridge, MA: MIT Press, 1992.

Singh, Simon. *Fermat's Enigma: The Epic Quest to Solve the World's Greatest Mathematical Problem.* New York: Walker and Co., 1997.

Thomas a Kempis, Sister Mary. "An Appreciation of Sophie Germain." *National Mathematics Magazine* 14, no. 2 (November 1939), 81-90.

Web sites

http://www.pbs.org/wgbh/nova/proof/germain.htm
The companion Web site to the *NOVA* episode "The Proof," about the quest to solve Fermat's Last Theorem, contains this profile of Sophie Germain and her work.

http://scienceworld.wolfram.com/biography/Germain.html
A short biography of Sophie Germain, with links to the scientific and mathematical fields to which she contributed.

http://www-groups.dcs.st-and.ac.uk/~history/Biographies/Germain.html
A biography of Sophie Germain, from the MacTutor History of Mathematics archive, maintained by the School of Mathematics and Statistics at the University of St. Andrews, Scotland.

Index